This Journal Belongs To

_____

_____

_____

Rennie and Sage
I Am Affirmation and Gratitude Journal:
A Daily Manifestation Guide
Text and images © 2023 Rennie and Sage

ISBN: 979-8-9891080-0-8

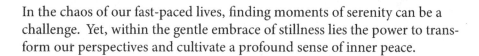

Introduction

In the chaos of our fast-paced lives, finding moments of serenity can be a challenge. Yet, within the gentle embrace of stillness lies the power to transform our perspectives and cultivate a profound sense of inner peace.

This journal is not just a collection of blank pages; it is a sacred space meticulously designed to lead you on a daily journey into the depths of your own being. Rooted in the philosophy that we can find serenity through stillness, this journal is a companion on your quest for self-discovery and inner calm.

Throughout these pages, you will embark on a mindful exploration of powerful "I Am" affirmations—a practice that transcends words and ventures into the realm of self-empowerment. Each affirmation serves as a compass, gently directing your focus inward, encouraging reflection, and inviting a sense of peace that can only be found in the stillness of the present moment.

Creating your "I Am" affirmation is a deeply personal and empowering process. Begin by settling into a quiet space where you can fully focus on your thoughts. Close your eyes, take a few deep breaths, and allow your mind to ease into a state of calm. Reflect on what you wish to cultivate within yourself and your life—be it strength, peace, resilience, abundance, or joy. Phrase your affirmation in the present tense, as if it is already a part of your reality. For example, instead of saying, "I will be confident," say, "I am confident." Keep it concise, specific, and positive.

Integrate gratitude into this daily practice. Express thankfulness for the qualities you already possess and those you aspire to cultivate. This infusion of gratitude adds a layer of appreciation, enhancing the transformative power of your affirmations.

Feel free to explore various aspects of your life, from relationships to personal goals, and frame each affirmation with intention and authenticity. Let the daily prompts inspire you, or tap into what you currently feel or desire. As you write, envision your ideal self, and let that vision guide every word. Revisit and revise your affirmations regularly, allowing them to evolve as you grow. Embrace this daily manifestation practice, and let the affirmations serve as gentle reminders of the serene stillness within you.

As you embark on this journey, consider this journal not as an obligation, but as an invitation to pause, breathe, and reconnect. Embrace the stillness, surrender to the process, and allow the power of "I Am" affirmations to unfold in the gentle rhythm of your everyday existence.

I am
choosing to create
a life that aligns
with my passions.

Describe the person I want to become in the next year.

Today I am grateful for:

Today's affirmation : I am...

List three specific goals I'm working towards manifesting.

Today I am grateful for:

Today's affirmation : I am...

I am finding joy in...

Today I am grateful for:

Today's affirmation : I am...

How can I incorporate mindfulness into my daily routine?

Today I am grateful for:

Today's affirmation : I am...

Describe a meaningful conversation I've had with someone recently.

Today I am grateful for:

Today's affirmation : I am...

Write about an activity or hobby that brings me pure happiness.

Today I am grateful for:

Today's affirmation : I am...

What's a goal I've achieved that I once thought was out of reach?

Today I am grateful for:

Today's affirmation : I am...

Describe a recent moment when I felt truly inspired.

Today I am grateful for:

Today's affirmation : I am...

How can I shift my perspective from challenges to opportunities?

Today I am grateful for:

Today's affirmation : I am...

Reflect on a past challenge and find something positive that came from it.

Today I am grateful for:

Today's affirmation : I am...

Describe my ideal day and manifest it in writing.

Today I am grateful for:

Today's affirmation : I am...

——— ——— ———

What activities bring me a sense of peace? How can I make time for them?

Today I am grateful for:

Today's affirmation : I am...

What strengths have I developed through past challenges?

Today I am grateful for:

Today's affirmation : I am...

Describe a moment of mindfulness I experienced today.

Today I am grateful for:

Today's affirmation : I am...

What are my values and do they align with my goals?

Today I am grateful for:

Today's affirmation : I am...

What qualities do I appreciate most about myself?

Today I am grateful for:

Today's affirmation : I am...

___ ___ ___

List three things I love about my surroundings right now.

Today I am grateful for:

Today's affirmation : I am...

How do I find stillness in the midst of a busy day?

Today I am grateful for:

Today's affirmation : I am...

Write about a time when I successfully manifested something into my life.

Today I am grateful for:

Today's affirmation : I am...

I am excited about...

Today I am grateful for:

Today's affirmation : I am...

I am surrounded by love and support because...

Today I am grateful for:

Today's affirmation : I am...

I am celebrating my achievements, including...

Today I am grateful for:

Today's affirmation : I am...

How can I show myself more compassion today?

Today I am grateful for:

Today's affirmation : I am...

Describe a recent moment that made me smile or brought me joy.

Today I am grateful for:

Today's affirmation : I am...

Describe a time when I pushed past my comfort zone and achieved something great.

Today I am grateful for:

Today's affirmation : I am...

Describe the impact of nature and the outdoors on my overall well-being.

Today I am grateful for:

Today's affirmation : I am...

Write about a role model or someone who inspires me to be a better person.

Today I am grateful for:

Today's affirmation : I am...

How can I practice active listening and show genuine interest in others?

Today I am grateful for:

Today's affirmation : I am...

Reflect on the times when I've laughed the hardest and what triggered it.

Today I am grateful for:

Today's affirmation : I am...

List the accomplishments I'm proud of in my personal and professional life.

Today I am grateful for:

Today's affirmation : I am...

How can I make space for creativity in my daily routine?

Today I am grateful for:

Today's affirmation : I am...

Describe a situation where I practiced patience and maintained a positive attitude.

Today I am grateful for:

Today's affirmation : I am...

What am I thankful for in my relationships?

Today I am grateful for:

Today's affirmation : I am...

What small thing can I do today to affirm my commitment to personal growth?

Today I am grateful for:

Today's affirmation : I am...

Envision a state of optimal health and well-being. What step(s) can I take toward it?

Today I am grateful for:

Today's affirmation : I am...

Describe my ideal self-care routine and commit to incorporating it into my week.

Today I am grateful for:

Today's affirmation : I am...

How do I handle stress, and are there healthier alternatives I can explore?

Today I am grateful for:

Today's affirmation : I am...

Write about the beauty I find in ordinary, everyday moments.

Today I am grateful for:

Today's affirmation : I am...

Write about a skill I want to develop and create a plan to work on it.

Today I am grateful for:

Today's affirmation : I am...

How can I use affirmations to boost my self-confidence today?

Today I am grateful for:

Today's affirmation : I am...

Express gratitude for the people who have positively influenced my life.

Today I am grateful for:

Today's affirmation : I am...

Write about a place or activity that makes me feel calm and centered.

Today I am grateful for:

Today's affirmation : I am...

Reflect on the power of belief in the manifestation process.

Today I am grateful for:

Today's affirmation : I am...

I am inspired by...

Today I am grateful for:

Today's affirmation : I am...

I am forgiving myself for...

Today I am grateful for:

Today's affirmation : I am...

I am expressing gratitude for my body because...

Today I am grateful for:

Today's affirmation : I am...

How can I spread kindness to others today?

Today I am grateful for:

Today's affirmation : I am...

How can I stay focused and motivated on my long-term goals?

Today I am grateful for:

Today's affirmation : I am...

Describe a recent moment when I felt fully present and mindful.

Today I am grateful for:

Today's affirmation : I am...

Write about a situation where I displayed resilience and determination.

Today I am grateful for:

Today's affirmation : I am...

Write about a time when I supported a friend or loved one in a meaningful way.

Today I am grateful for:

Today's affirmation : I am...

What's a simple pleasure that never fails to make me happy?

Today I am grateful for:

Today's affirmation : I am...

How can I shift my mindset to focus on abundance rather than scarcity?

Today I am grateful for:

Today's affirmation : I am...

Write about a project or idea I'm excited to pursue.

Today I am grateful for:

Today's affirmation : I am...

How can I surround myself with positive influences and uplifting content?

Today I am grateful for:

Today's affirmation : I am...

Write about a place I'm grateful to have visited or lived.

Today I am grateful for:

Today's affirmation : I am...

Affirm my capacity to create positive change.

Today I am grateful for:

Today's affirmation : I am...

Envision a successful outcome for a project I'm working on.

Today I am grateful for:

Today's affirmation : I am...

Write about a self-care practice that always boosts my mood.

Today I am grateful for:

Today's affirmation : I am...

How has my perspective on life evolved over the years?

Today I am grateful for:

Today's affirmation : I am...

Practice gratitude for my senses. What am I thankful for seeing, hearing, smelling, tasting, and touching?

Today I am grateful for:

Today's affirmation : I am...

Describe a moment of stillness that brought me peace recently.

Today I am grateful for:

Today's affirmation : I am...

Reflect on a challenging situation; is there something positive to be found in it?

Today I am grateful for:

Today's affirmation : I am...

Reflect on the sights and sounds of nature that bring me tranquility.

Today I am grateful for:

Today's affirmation : I am...

Describe the emotions I will feel when my manifestations come to fruition.

Today I am grateful for:

Today's affirmation : I am...

I am letting go of...

Today I am grateful for:

Today's affirmation : I am...

I am deserving of...

Today I am grateful for:

Today's affirmation : I am...

I am setting boundaries with...

Today I am grateful for:

Today's affirmation : I am...

_____   _____   _____

I am attracting abundance in my life because...

Today I am grateful for:

Today's affirmation : I am...

_____   _____   _____

I am letting go of regrets about...

Today I am grateful for:

Today's affirmation : I am...

I am finding joy in the little things, like...

Today I am grateful for:

Today's affirmation : I am...

I am grateful for the support I receive from...

Today I am grateful for:

Today's affirmation : I am...

I am embracing my unique path, even if it means...

Today I am grateful for:

Today's affirmation : I am...

I am finding balance in my life by...

Today I am grateful for:

Today's affirmation : I am...

I am committed to my personal development in...

Today I am grateful for:

Today's affirmation : I am...

What are three things I love about myself?

Today I am grateful for:

Today's affirmation : I am...

How can I find positivity in difficult situations?

Today I am grateful for:

Today's affirmation : I am...

What are my top three short-term goals?

Today I am grateful for:

Today's affirmation : I am...

Write about a lesson I've learned from a difficult experience.

Today I am grateful for:

Today's affirmation : I am...

List three areas in which I've shown improvement and growth recently.

Today I am grateful for:

Today's affirmation : I am...

How can I foster deeper connections with the people I care about?

Today I am grateful for:

Today's affirmation : I am...

Describe a memory that always brings a smile to my face.

Today I am grateful for:

Today's affirmation : I am...

Write about a time when taking a risk led to a rewarding outcome.

Today I am grateful for:

Today's affirmation : I am...

Write about a quote or piece of art that resonates deeply with me.

Today I am grateful for:

Today's affirmation : I am...

_____ _____ _____

How are positive affirmations empowering me?

Today I am grateful for:

Today's affirmation : I am...

Write about a happy memory from my childhood.

Today I am grateful for:

Today's affirmation : I am...

What positive qualities do others see in me?

Today I am grateful for:

Today's affirmation : I am...

Manifest a positive shift in a challenging situation I'm facing.

Today I am grateful for:

Today's affirmation : I am...

How can I prioritize self-care today?

Today I am grateful for:

Today's affirmation : I am...

Write a note to my past self, offering words of wisdom and encouragement.

Today I am grateful for:

Today's affirmation : I am...

Reflect on a time when I felt truly present and engaged in the moment.

Today I am grateful for:

Today's affirmation : I am...

What is my biggest strength? How can I leverage it in pursuing my goals?

Today I am grateful for:

Today's affirmation : I am...

What feeling resonates with me most today?

Today I am grateful for:

Today's affirmation : I am...

What aspects of nature am I grateful for today?

Today I am grateful for:

Today's affirmation : I am...

Who can I make laugh today?

Today I am grateful for:

Today's affirmation : I am...

How can I incorporate moments of stillness into my daily routine?

Today I am grateful for:

Today's affirmation : I am...

Visualize an element I want to go well today; describe it in detail.

Today I am grateful for:

Today's affirmation : I am...

How can gratitude enhance the manifestation of my desires?

Today I am grateful for:

Today's affirmation : I am...

I am proud of...

Today I am grateful for:

Today's affirmation : I am...

I am at peace with...

Today I am grateful for:

Today's affirmation : I am...

_____ __ _____

I am learning to...

Today I am grateful for:

Today's affirmation : I am...

_____ __ _____

I am in control of...

Today I am grateful for:

Today's affirmation : I am...

I am dedicated to my growth in...

Today I am grateful for:

Today's affirmation : I am...

I am letting go of negative self-talk about...

Today I am grateful for:

Today's affirmation : I am...

I am confident in my ability to handle...

Today I am grateful for:

Today's affirmation : I am...

I am trusting the process of...

Today I am grateful for:

Today's affirmation : I am...

I am manifesting positivity by...

Today I am grateful for:

Today's affirmation : I am...

I am valuing my time and energy by...

Today I am grateful for:

Today's affirmation : I am...

I am becoming more resilient in the face of...

Today I am grateful for:

Today's affirmation : I am...

List five achievements I'm proud of, no matter how small.

Today I am grateful for:

Today's affirmation : I am...

Write about a person in my life who brings positivity and how they impact me.

Today I am grateful for:

Today's affirmation : I am...

_____   _____   _____

Write about a characteristic I want to develop further.

Today I am grateful for:

Today's affirmation : I am...

What is a positive phrase I can use to center myself throughout the day?

Today I am grateful for:

Today's affirmation : I am...

How can I step out of my comfort zone today?

Today I am grateful for:

Today's affirmation : I am...

Reflect on the qualities that make me a good friend or partner.

Today I am grateful for:

Today's affirmation : I am...

How can I infuse more joy and lightheartedness into my day?

Today I am grateful for:

Today's affirmation : I am...

___ ___ _____

What steps can I take to attract more opportunities and success into my life?

Today I am grateful for:

Today's affirmation : I am...

How can I be creative today?

Today I am grateful for:

Today's affirmation : I am...

Three things that I feel hopeful about are...

Today I am grateful for:

Today's affirmation : I am...

Is there something I can change my mindset on that might lead to a positive outcome?

Today I am grateful for:

Today's affirmation : I am...

Express gratitude for a specific skill or talent I possess.

Today I am grateful for:

Today's affirmation : I am...

What do I need to hear right now?

Today I am grateful for:

Today's affirmation : I am...

Write about the kind of energy I want to attract into my life.

Today I am grateful for:

Today's affirmation : I am...

List three things I love about myself.

Today I am grateful for:

Today's affirmation : I am...

Reflect on a recent obstacle and identify the lesson it taught me.

Today I am grateful for:

Today's affirmation : I am...

Describe the feeling of being fully immersed in an activity I love.

Today I am grateful for:

Today's affirmation : I am...

What is my greatest fear?

Today I am grateful for:

Today's affirmation : I am...

Describe a recent achievement; how can I celebrate it?

Today I am grateful for:

Today's affirmation : I am...

Reflect on a time when I overcame a fear and felt empowered.

Today I am grateful for:

Today's affirmation : I am...

——— — ——— ———

List three small pleasures in my day.

Today I am grateful for:

Today's affirmation : I am...

Describe the feeling of complete serenity; how can I invite it into my life today?

Today I am grateful for:

Today's affirmation : I am...

Explore the concept of letting go and allowing manifestations to unfold.

Today I am grateful for:

Today's affirmation : I am...

I am confident in...

Today I am grateful for:

Today's affirmation : I am...

I am open to...

Today I am grateful for:

Today's affirmation : I am...

I am focusing my energy on...

Today I am grateful for:

Today's affirmation : I am...

I am acknowledging my self-worth because...

Today I am grateful for:

Today's affirmation : I am...

I am taking steps towards...

Today I am grateful for:

Today's affirmation : I am...

I am envisioning a future where...

Today I am grateful for:

Today's affirmation : I am...

I am choosing to focus on the positives of...

Today I am grateful for:

Today's affirmation : I am...

I am learning to say no to...

Today I am grateful for:

Today's affirmation : I am...

I am finding strength in vulnerability by...

Today I am grateful for:

Today's affirmation : I am...

I am letting go of guilt related to...

Today I am grateful for:

Today's affirmation : I am...

I am choosing love over fear when it comes to...

Today I am grateful for:

Today's affirmation : I am...

How can I nurture my body and mind today?

Today I am grateful for:

Today's affirmation : I am...

What's something I often take for granted that I'm thankful for?

Today I am grateful for:

Today's affirmation : I am...

——— ——— ———

What one step can I take today to bring me closer to my dreams?

Today I am grateful for:

Today's affirmation : I am...

Write a note to my future self, detailing the life I want to lead.

Today I am grateful for:

Today's affirmation : I am...

How can I cultivate a positive self-image and boost my self-confidence?

Today I am grateful for:

Today's affirmation : I am...

What are some ways I can express gratitude and appreciation to those around me?

Today I am grateful for:

Today's affirmation : I am...

What's a goal I can set to bring more happiness into my life?

Today I am grateful for:

Today's affirmation : I am...

Reflect on how far I've come in achieving my financial goals.

Today I am grateful for:

Today's affirmation : I am...

Describe a person who embodies the creativity and passion I admire.

Today I am grateful for:

Today's affirmation : I am...

What's a negative thought pattern I can replace with a more positive one?

Today I am grateful for:

Today's affirmation : I am...

What aspects of nature do I enjoy the most?

Today I am grateful for:

Today's affirmation : I am...

What can I do today to empower myself in my work or studies?

Today I am grateful for:

Today's affirmation : I am...

Write my top goal as if it's already been achieved.

Today I am grateful for:

Today's affirmation : I am...

Reflect on a recent success and celebrate it as an act of self-care.

Today I am grateful for:

Today's affirmation : I am...

Write about a role model or mentor who has positively influenced my life.

Today I am grateful for:

Today's affirmation : I am...

Write about a mindful breathing exercise that helps me center myself.

Today I am grateful for:

Today's affirmation : I am...

Write about a challenge I'm currently facing and brainstorm solutions.

Today I am grateful for:

Today's affirmation : I am...

What technique can I use to empower me in times of stress?

Today I am grateful for:

Today's affirmation : I am...

Write about a past experience that taught me a valuable lesson and express gratitude for the lesson.

Today I am grateful for:

Today's affirmation : I am...

Explore the idea of mental stillness. How can I quiet my mind?

Today I am grateful for:

Today's affirmation : I am...

Write a manifestation note to the universe outlining my deepest desires.

Today I am grateful for:

Today's affirmation : I am...

I am embracing...

Today I am grateful for:

Today's affirmation : I am...

I am radiating positivity because...

Today I am grateful for:

Today's affirmation : I am...

I am becoming more aware of...

Today I am grateful for:

Today's affirmation : I am...

I am becoming a better version of myself by...

Today I am grateful for:

Today's affirmation : I am...

I am discovering my purpose in...

Today I am grateful for:

Today's affirmation : I am...

I am open to receiving...

Today I am grateful for:

Today's affirmation : I am...

I am recognizing the abundance in my life, such as...

Today I am grateful for:

Today's affirmation : I am...

What positive words would I use to describe myself?

Today I am grateful for:

Today's affirmation : I am...

Write about a place that always brings me peace and happiness.

Today I am grateful for:

Today's affirmation : I am...

Reflect on past accomplishments and how they've shaped my journey.

Today I am grateful for:

Today's affirmation : I am...

Reflect on how far I've come since the beginning of the year.

Today I am grateful for:

Today's affirmation : I am...

What are my strengths and how can I celebrate them today?

Today I am grateful for:

Today's affirmation : I am...

Describe a person who has positively influenced my life journey.

Today I am grateful for:

Today's affirmation : I am...

_____ _____ _____

Describe a moment when I felt genuinely content and at peace.

Today I am grateful for:

Today's affirmation : I am...

How can I overcome self-limiting beliefs that might be holding me back?

Today I am grateful for:

Today's affirmation : I am...

Reflect on the times when I've overcome creative blocks and found inspiration.

Today I am grateful for:

Today's affirmation : I am...

Write about a time when I successfully re-framed a difficult situation.

Today I am grateful for:

Today's affirmation : I am...

List three things about my current situation that I appreciate.

Today I am grateful for:

Today's affirmation : I am...

Affirm my worthiness of love and joy.

Today I am grateful for:

Today's affirmation : I am...

Manifest a sense of peace and calm for the week ahead.

Today I am grateful for:

Today's affirmation : I am...

What boundaries do I need to set to protect my well-being?

Today I am grateful for:

Today's affirmation : I am...

Reflect on a time when I overcame self-doubt and achieved success.

Today I am grateful for:

Today's affirmation : I am...

How can I bring more mindfulness into my daily routine?

Today I am grateful for:

Today's affirmation : I am...

What achievements, big or small, am I grateful for in my life?

Today I am grateful for:

Today's affirmation : I am...

Write about a mindful practice that brings me peace.

Today I am grateful for:

Today's affirmation : I am...

Reflect on the progress I've made towards manifesting a particular goal.

Today I am grateful for:

Today's affirmation : I am...

I am strong enough to...

Today I am grateful for:

Today's affirmation : I am...

I am kind to myself when...

Today I am grateful for:

Today's affirmation : I am...

I am making space for...

Today I am grateful for:

Today's affirmation : I am...

I am honoring my inner wisdom by...

Today I am grateful for:

Today's affirmation : I am...

I am taking action on my dreams by...

Today I am grateful for:

Today's affirmation : I am...

I am trusting myself to make decisions about...

Today I am grateful for:

Today's affirmation : I am...

I am finding meaning and purpose in...

Today I am grateful for:

Today's affirmation : I am...

Write a note to my younger self, offering words of encouragement.

Today I am grateful for:

Today's affirmation : I am...

What's a small achievement from today that I can celebrate?

Today I am grateful for:

Today's affirmation : I am...

Visualize a successful outcome for a challenge I'm currently facing.

Today I am grateful for:

Today's affirmation : I am...

What's a hobby or activity that brings me joy and helps me stay present?

Today I am grateful for:

Today's affirmation : I am...

Reflect on the times when I've overcome self-doubt and proven myself wrong.

Today I am grateful for:

Today's affirmation : I am...

How can I create a balance between my personal goals and maintaining relationships?

Today I am grateful for:

Today's affirmation : I am...

How can I prioritize doing things that bring me joy, even on busy days?

Today I am grateful for:

Today's affirmation : I am...

Describe the skills and qualities that have contributed to my successes.

Today I am grateful for:

Today's affirmation : I am...

How can I use my creativity to make a positive impact on the world?

Today I am grateful for:

Today's affirmation : I am...

What's a goal I can set to cultivate a consistently positive mindset?

Today I am grateful for:

Today's affirmation : I am...

Who has supported me recently, and how can I show gratitude?

Today I am grateful for:

Today's affirmation : I am...

Affirm your resilience in the face of adversity.

Today I am grateful for:

Today's affirmation : I am...

Visualize achieving a long-term goal and describe the emotions associated with it.

Today I am grateful for:

Today's affirmation : I am...

Write about a book, movie, or activity that brings me joy and plan to engage with it soon.

Today I am grateful for:

Today's affirmation : I am...

Reflect on a recent decision and its impact on my life.

Today I am grateful for:

Today's affirmation : I am...

Reflect on the impact of technology on my life and consider a digital detox.

Today I am grateful for:

Today's affirmation : I am...

What steps can I take to turn a big dream into a tangible goal?

Today I am grateful for:

Today's affirmation : I am...

Choose an area of my life that needs improvement; what is one small thing I can do today towards that improvement?

Today I am grateful for:

Today's affirmation : I am...

Reflect on the positive impact of a challenging person or situation in my life.

Today I am grateful for:

Today's affirmation : I am...

Reflect on the benefits of embracing stillness in my life.

Today I am grateful for:

Today's affirmation : I am...

Write a mantra for manifesting abundance in all areas of my life.

Today I am grateful for:

Today's affirmation : I am...

I am celebrating my progress in...

Today I am grateful for:

Today's affirmation : I am...

I am prioritizing self-care by...

Today I am grateful for:

Today's affirmation : I am...

I am allowing myself to rest when...

Today I am grateful for:

Today's affirmation : I am...

I am cultivating gratitude for my...

Today I am grateful for:

Today's affirmation : I am...

I am forgiving myself for not...

Today I am grateful for:

Today's affirmation : I am...

I am practicing gratitude for my unique gifts, such as...

Today I am grateful for:

Today's affirmation : I am...

I am evolving and growing because...

Today I am grateful for:

Today's affirmation : I am...

What are three things that make me unique and special?

Today I am grateful for:

Today's affirmation : I am...

Reflect on a past challenge I've overcome and the strength it gave me.

Today I am grateful for:

Today's affirmation : I am...

_____   _____   _____

What's one fear I can overcome to help me achieve my goals?

Today I am grateful for:

Today's affirmation : I am...

How can I release stress and tension from my mind and body right now?

Today I am grateful for:

Today's affirmation : I am...

_____ _____ _____

What's a challenge I've been avoiding that I can tackle with confidence?

Today I am grateful for:

Today's affirmation : I am...

Write a note to someone who has had a positive impact on my life.

Today I am grateful for:

Today's affirmation : I am...

Write about a place that holds special meaning and happy memories.

Today I am grateful for:

Today's affirmation : I am...

Write about a time when hard work and persistence paid off.

Today I am grateful for:

Today's affirmation : I am...

What's a new skill or hobby I can explore to ignite my creativity?

Today I am grateful for:

Today's affirmation : I am...

How can I start my day with positivity and intention?

Today I am grateful for:

Today's affirmation : I am...

——— ——— ———

Who in my life am I grateful to have as a role model?

Today I am grateful for:

Today's affirmation : I am...

Why is cultivating inner peace important to me?

Today I am grateful for:

Today's affirmation : I am...

Write a manifestation for increased confidence in a specific area of my life.

Today I am grateful for:

Today's affirmation : I am...

How can I infuse more playfulness into my life?

Today I am grateful for:

Today's affirmation : I am...

What personal values are most important to me, and how do I embody them?

Today I am grateful for:

Today's affirmation : I am...

Describe a place where I feel a deep sense of peace and tranquility.

Today I am grateful for:

Today's affirmation : I am...

Set a new goal for personal or professional growth and outline the first steps.

Today I am grateful for:

Today's affirmation : I am...

How can I re-frame a negative thought into a positive affirmation?

Today I am grateful for:

Today's affirmation : I am...

Write a gratitude note to myself for my accomplishments and growth.

Today I am grateful for:

Today's affirmation : I am...

What role does gratitude play in achieving inner serenity?

Today I am grateful for:

Today's affirmation : I am...

I am responsible for...

Today I am grateful for:

Today's affirmation : I am...

I am grateful for the lessons I've learned from...

Today I am grateful for:

Today's affirmation : I am...

I am letting go of fear related to...

Today I am grateful for:

Today's affirmation : I am...

I am channeling my energy into...

Today I am grateful for:

Today's affirmation : I am...

I am acknowledging my progress in...

Today I am grateful for:

Today's affirmation : I am...

I am practicing self-love by...

Today I am grateful for:

Today's affirmation : I am...

I am letting go of the need for perfection in...

Today I am grateful for:

Today's affirmation : I am...

I am finding peace in the chaos of...

Today I am grateful for:

Today's affirmation : I am...

Describe a recent situation where I handled challenges gracefully.

Today I am grateful for:

Today's affirmation : I am...

Describe the person I want to become in the next year, both internally and externally.

Today I am grateful for:

Today's affirmation : I am...

Describe the emotions and sensations I experience when I practice gratitude.

Today I am grateful for:

Today's affirmation : I am...

How can I celebrate my achievements without downplaying them?

Today I am grateful for:

Today's affirmation : I am...

What can I do to bring more positivity and warmth into my relationships?

Today I am grateful for:

Today's affirmation : I am...

What's a way I can spread positivity and happiness to those around me today?

Today I am grateful for:

Today's affirmation : I am...

_____   _____   _____

How can I celebrate my achievements and milestones with gratitude?

Today I am grateful for:

Today's affirmation : I am...

How can I share my creative journey with others and inspire them?

Today I am grateful for:

Today's affirmation : I am...

Describe the impact of maintaining a positive outlook on my overall well-being.

Today I am grateful for:

Today's affirmation : I am...

Express gratitude for the simple pleasures in my daily life.

Today I am grateful for:

Today's affirmation : I am...

Manifest abundance in my life.

Today I am grateful for:

Today's affirmation : I am...

Describe my dream home and the feelings associated with it.

Today I am grateful for:

Today's affirmation : I am...

Describe a self-care ritual I can start today.

Today I am grateful for:

Today's affirmation : I am...

Write about a goal I achieved and the steps I took to get there.

Today I am grateful for:

Today's affirmation : I am...

Practice mindful eating. Describe the flavors, textures, and sensations.

Today I am grateful for:

Today's affirmation : I am...

Write an affirmation for attracting peace and calm into my life.

Today I am grateful for:

Today's affirmation : I am...

Express gratitude for the opportunities that lie ahead.

Today I am grateful for:

Today's affirmation : I am...

I am motivated to...

Today I am grateful for:

Today's affirmation : I am...

I am accepting myself unconditionally because...

Today I am grateful for:

Today's affirmation : I am...

I am releasing old patterns of...

Today I am grateful for:

Today's affirmation : I am...

I am letting go of comparison with...

Today I am grateful for:

Today's affirmation : I am...

I am setting intentions for...

Today I am grateful for:

Today's affirmation : I am...

What's a mistake I've made that I can now view as a valuable learning experience?

Today I am grateful for:

Today's affirmation : I am...

How can I acknowledge and celebrate my progress, no matter how small?

Today I am grateful for:

Today's affirmation : I am...

What qualities do I appreciate in myself?

Today I am grateful for:

Today's affirmation : I am...

Affirm my ability to overcome challenges.

Today I am grateful for:

Today's affirmation : I am...

Manifest a healthy work-life balance.

Today I am grateful for:

Today's affirmation : I am...

What is a small act of kindness I can do for myself right now?

Today I am grateful for:

Today's affirmation : I am...

Reflect on a time when I stepped out of my comfort zone and grew.

Today I am grateful for:

Today's affirmation : I am...

Write about a mindfulness or meditation practice that resonates with me.

Today I am grateful for:

Today's affirmation : I am...

Create an affirmation for overcoming a current challenge I'm facing.

Today I am grateful for:

Today's affirmation : I am...

I am making a difference by...

Today I am grateful for:

Today's affirmation : I am...

I am embracing my unique qualities, such as...

Today I am grateful for:

Today's affirmation : I am...

I am becoming more patient with...

Today I am grateful for:

Today's affirmation : I am...

I am attracting positive relationships because...

Today I am grateful for:

Today's affirmation : I am...

How can I prioritize self-care in my daily routine?

Today I am grateful for:

Today's affirmation : I am...

Write a sentence that celebrates my strengths.

Today I am grateful for:

Today's affirmation : I am...

Describe the person I want to become and manifest those qualities.

Today I am grateful for:

Today's affirmation : I am...

Reflect on a challenge and brainstorm self-care strategies to navigate it.

Today I am grateful for:

Today's affirmation : I am...

What are my top priorities in life, and are they reflected in my daily actions?

Today I am grateful for:

Today's affirmation : I am...

How can I cultivate a sense of presence in my interactions with others today?

Today I am grateful for:

Today's affirmation : I am...

Is there a recent setback I've experienced that I can turn into a stepping stone toward success?

Today I am grateful for:

Today's affirmation : I am...

What affirmations align with my goals and aspirations?

Today I am grateful for:

Today's affirmation : I am...

I am practicing self-compassion by...

Today I am grateful for:

Today's affirmation : I am...

I am seeking opportunities to...

Today I am grateful for:

Today's affirmation : I am...

I am accepting the past and moving forward with...

Today I am grateful for:

Today's affirmation : I am...

I am creating a life filled with...

Today I am grateful for:

Today's affirmation : I am...

_____ _____ _____

I am appreciating the beauty of...

Today I am grateful for:

Today's affirmation : I am...

_____ _____ _____

I am letting go of negative influences like...

Today I am grateful for:

Today's affirmation : I am...

I am attracting positivity into my life by...

Today I am grateful for:

Today's affirmation : I am...

List five things I can see, hear, or feel right now.

Today I am grateful for:

Today's affirmation : I am...

Reflect on a recent accomplishment and express gratitude for the journey.

Today I am grateful for:

Today's affirmation : I am...

Repeat an affirmation that centers around self-love.

Today I am grateful for:

Today's affirmation : I am...

Write about a dream or aspiration I want to manifest into reality today.

Today I am grateful for:

Today's affirmation : I am...

Write about an activity that makes me feel truly alive.

Today I am grateful for:

Today's affirmation : I am...

Write about a moment that made me feel proud of who I am.

Today I am grateful for:

Today's affirmation : I am...

Reflect on the beauty of impermanence and the constant flow of life.

Today I am grateful for:

Today's affirmation : I am...

I am attracting positivity into my life by...

Today I am grateful for:

Today's affirmation : I am...

I am committed to improving my...

Today I am grateful for:

Today's affirmation : I am...

I am showing myself love by...

Today I am grateful for:

Today's affirmation : I am...

I am becoming more mindful of...

Today I am grateful for:

Today's affirmation : I am...

I am making space for growth by...

Today I am grateful for:

Today's affirmation : I am...

I am embracing the unknown by...

Today I am grateful for:

Today's affirmation : I am...

I am making space for growth by...

Today I am grateful for...

Today's affirmation: I am...

I am letting the unhealthy...

...am grateful for...

Today's affirmation: I am...

Express thanks for a lesson I've learned recently.

Today I am grateful for:

Today's affirmation : I am...

Affirm my belief in my ability to attract positive opportunities.

Today I am grateful for:

Today's affirmation : I am...

Manifest a positive change in a relationship I'm currently navigating.

Today I am grateful for:

Today's affirmation : I am...

How do I nourish my mind, body, and spirit on a daily basis?

Today I am grateful for:

Today's affirmation : I am...

How do I define success, and how has that definition changed over time?

Today I am grateful for:

Today's affirmation : I am...

Write about a mindful movement practice that connects me to my body.

Today I am grateful for:

Today's affirmation : I am...

I am capable of...

Today I am grateful for:

Today's affirmation : I am...

I am embracing change by...

Today I am grateful for:

Today's affirmation : I am...

I am recognizing my inner strength in dealing with...

Today I am grateful for:

Today's affirmation : I am...

I am empowering myself by...

Today I am grateful for:

Today's affirmation : I am...

Express gratitude for the power of positive affirmations.

Today I am grateful for:

Today's affirmation : I am...

Manifest a strong sense of purpose and fulfillment.

Today I am grateful for:

Today's affirmation : I am...

How do I know when I'm starting to feel burnt out and what can I do about it?

Today I am grateful for:

Today's affirmation : I am...

List three mantras for self-compassion.

Today I am grateful for:

Today's affirmation : I am...

Reflect on a relationship that has taught me valuable lessons.

Today I am grateful for:

Today's affirmation : I am...

Describe the sensation of being fully grounded in the present moment.

Today I am grateful for:

Today's affirmation : I am...

Describe a unique gift I have that I can share with others.

Today I am grateful for:

Today's affirmation : I am...

I am embracing the present moment by...

Today I am grateful for:

Today's affirmation : I am...

List three small goals for today.

Today I am grateful for:

Today's affirmation : I am...

I am finding beauty in...

Today I am grateful for:

Today's affirmation : I am...

I am letting go of self-doubt in relation to...

Today I am grateful for:

Today's affirmation : I am...

What small act of kindness can I commit to today?

Today I am grateful for:

Today's affirmation : I am...

What is my favorite song? Listen to it today.

Today I am grateful for:

Today's affirmation : I am...

Is there a task I've been putting off that I can do today?

Today I am grateful for:

Today's affirmation : I am...

_____ _____ _____

What is my favorite food?

Today I am grateful for:

Today's affirmation : I am...

This week, I hope to...

Today I am grateful for:

Today's affirmation : I am...

What do I want to be remembered for?

Today I am grateful for:

Today's affirmation : I am...

When and where do I feel the most safe?

Today I am grateful for:

Today's affirmation : I am...

What has been the hardest thing to let go of in my life?

Today I am grateful for:

Today's affirmation : I am...

What is my top priority for today?

Today I am grateful for:

Today's affirmation : I am...

Is there something I would like to do less often?

Today I am grateful for:

Today's affirmation : I am...

What is my happiest memory from this week?

Today I am grateful for:

Today's affirmation : I am...

Write about my favorite season.

Today I am grateful for:

Today's affirmation : I am...

Is there something I am feeling insecure about?

Today I am grateful for:

Today's affirmation : I am...

Describe the last time I laughed.

Today I am grateful for:

Today's affirmation : I am...

What makes me feel loved and valued?

Today I am grateful for:

Today's affirmation : I am...

Describe a place I'd love to visit.

Today I am grateful for:

Today's affirmation : I am...

Describe myself in five words.

Today I am grateful for:

Today's affirmation : I am...

What is something I never get tired of talking about?

Today I am grateful for:

Today's affirmation : I am...

Is there anyone I need to apologize to?

Today I am grateful for:

Today's affirmation : I am...

What book(s) do I want to read?

Today I am grateful for:

Today's affirmation : I am...

Today I want to feel...

Today I am grateful for:

Today's affirmation : I am...

Describe my sleep routine.

Today I am grateful for:

Today's affirmation : I am...

_____ _____ _____

What am I most excited for right now?

Today I am grateful for:

Today's affirmation : I am...

What cause(s) am I passionate about?

Today I am grateful for:

Today's affirmation : I am...

What makes me a good friend?

Today I am grateful for:

Today's affirmation : I am...

What am I proud of myself for today?

Today I am grateful for:

Today's affirmation : I am...

Where do I want to be in five years?

Today I am grateful for:

Today's affirmation : I am...

How have I grown as a person in the last year?

Today I am grateful for:

Today's affirmation : I am...

Made in the USA
Monee, IL
26 November 2024

71303346R00203